The Royal Children

To children everywhere

TheROYAL CHILDREN

Ian Digby

Leslie Frewin : London

© Leslie Frewin Publishers Limited, 1967
First published by Leslie Frewin Publishers Limited,
15 Hay's Mews, Berkeley Square, London W1.
This book is set in Garamond,
printed by Anchor Press and
bound by William Brendon,
both of Tiptree, Essex.

Acknowledgements

The Publishers would like to thank the following
for their co-operation in supplying the illustrations
for this book :
Keystone Press
Syndication International
Central Press
Press Association
Fox Photos
Studio Lisa
Newnes and Pearson

Special thanks go to Mr Edward Wing, the major
contributor of photographs.

Introduction

Within the last few years of this, Britain's second Elizabethan era, the British Royal Family has experienced something of a population explosion. In six years there have been eight additions to the line of succession to the throne.

For the first time since pre-war days the Royal homes of Britain are echoing with the screams, shouts, tantrums and laughter of a new generation of Royal children.

This book pictures the babies of the sixties, from Prince Andrew, the Queen's third child, to Miss Marina Ogilvy, Princess Alexandra's daughter, and takes a fresh look at their brothers, sisters and cousins – from Prince Charles, the Prince of Wales, to Robert Lascelles, third son of the Earl of Harewood.

Its brief is confined to children of the immediate Royal Family and therefore early in line of succession; and to the legal definition of a child – those under the age of 21.

These, then, are the Royal Children, in order of succession to the throne:

Prince Charles, Prince of Wales

Born 14th November 1948

SCORPIO – Shrewd, tenacious, firm, determined, frank, energetic, and loyal.

CHARLES PHILIP ARTHUR GEORGE, who started his first year at Trinity College, Cambridge, a few weeks before his nineteenth birthday, is, of course, the heir apparent to his mother's throne. It is this fact that has creased the brows of the Royal pundits, has sent them tut-tutting into print and comment, and has had them wagging warning fingers at the prospect.

They are worried that Charles will suffer the same fate as did his great-great-grandfather, King Edward VII, when he was Prince of Wales. Edward VII, who also went to Trinity, had to wait in the wings more than forty years before ascending the throne. And while he was waiting, the pundits point out, Edward did not always adhere to the Royal textbook on how a Prince of Wales should conduct himself. It is quite possible, of course, that Charles may have to wait until the year 2000 – more than thirty years – he becomes King. But there is no justifiable reason to suggest that this will have a detrimental effect on him, or, indeed, that he will allow it to. The pundits, surely, have reckoned without Charles himself and an era that is very, very different from Victorian days.

Charles is a talented young man – a fact that has not always registered with his public. He may not be academically brilliant, although his record so far is well up to the national average – five passes at the GCE Ordinary Level and two at Advance. He may not have the dash or panache of his father, Prince Philip – showman qualities that the British, after preliminary suspicion, readily appreciate in their leaders. He may not have a particularly imposing or regal appearance – what teenager does? – nor is he particularly good-looking or striking according to the dictates of current fashion.

But he is an earnest, hard-working, industrious young man; serious, sensitive, considerate and a self-acknowledged introvert. He is only now overcoming an innate shyness with strangers, particularly those of his own age. In the last two years or so, during which

he has tasted responsibility for the first time – 'Guardian', or head boy, at Gordonstoun, for instance – he has matured considerably and assumed a new air of confidence.

He has a particular inclination towards the arts and is a good actor and singer – 'one of the best at Gordonstoun' – appearing as the Pirate King in a school production of *The Pirates of Penzance* and in the title role in *Macbeth*.

He has been studying the cello for a little more than a year and after only seven months was described by his tutor as 'quite brilliant'. He is also something of an accomplished trumpet player and flautist.

These are not attributes that meet with widespread public approval or admiration. Today they would be classed as 'square' and it is in this reaction that Charles faces his greatest challenge.

It is probably true to say that the vast majority of young people in Britain are totally indifferent to the monarchy. Few under thirty years of age can remember the patriotism of the war years when 'King and Country' meant so much. And none can recall the Jingoism, and all associated with it, of earlier years. To some, the Royal Family are an expensive luxury, a group of aloof, not particularly engaging, personalities, about whom it is difficult to hold any positive opinion, unless it be that the system sustaining them should be abolished. Prince Philip, perhaps, is the one exception to this attitude, and possibly Lord Snowdon – but then he was born plain MISTER Armstrong-Jones.

Philip is very concerned that Charles should have the qualities that will appeal to his public because he, Philip, must be well aware of this attitude. He may also be well aware that the main responsibility for restoring the monarchy in the hearts of youth lies with Charles.

The Prince of Wales has an enormous task. He is widely regarded by younger people – or at least by those who have an opinion to offer – as an ineffectual, pallid personality, lacking in character, substance and drive. That this opinion is based only on gossip and the occasional unflattering newspaper photograph is not particularly relevant. What matters perhaps is, Charles has no tangible way of correcting this delusion. He is entirely at the mercy of the popular whim which, at the moment, subconsciously compares him with his father – unfavourably.

Charles, however, has never been lacking in character. Shy and a little reticent, yes, but he's been through all the usual boyhood and teenage capers. The occasional one has escaped through the privacy which has been wrapped round him by Palace protocol and has shown him to be very much a boy of character and spirit.

There was, of course, the cherry brandy incident and the occasion when President Eisenhower, as he then was, visited Balmoral. He presented Charles with a handsome pen-stand and Charles, out of gratitude and the desire to reciprocate in some small way, decided on a line of action that demonstrated both initiative and a charming sense of humour.

With the help of a Castle footman he raided the office of the Controller of Supplies at Balmoral, obtained some stiff cardboard, moulded it into the shape of lapel badges, wrote 'I like Ike' on them and persuaded several members of the household to join him in wearing one throughout Eisenhower's visit.

His relationship with Princess Anne is another pointer to his developing maturity. In earlier years she used to tease him and he sometimes found it difficult to resist without losing his patience. During a stay at Sandringham Charles received a go-kart as a gift. Philip showed him and Anne how to drive it by taking it on a circuit of the paths behind the castle. Anne insisted on trying it next and, apparently, drove on and on, refusing to stop for Charles to drive. Charles found it hard to control his temper and when at last Anne did stop, he jumped into the kart in a fit of pique – and drove it straight into a rose bush.

But now, it seems, Charles does not get rattled when Anne, on fewer and fewer occasions, teases him a little.

Charles is maturing fast and after a year or more at Cambridge – he is studying archaeology and anthropology – possibly another at a Commonwealth university, although, as yet, there has been no firm indication of this, and service in one of the armed forces – most probably the Navy – he should be well prepared for the task ahead of him: to restore the dwindling faith of the British in their monarchy.

Prince Andrew

Born 19th February 1960

AQUARIUS – humane, lover of freedom, progressive, sensitive, altruistic and perhaps slightly bohemian.

ANDREW ALBERT CHRISTIAN EDWARD probably takes more after his father, Prince Philip, than either of his brothers. In the words of one of the staff at Buckingham Palace, 'he's a real ball of fire . . . keen-eyed, vigorous and always on the move'. In a short time he has established himself as an impish but lovable character. He is a very sturdy, chunky little boy, well built, with plenty of energy and stamina. He thoroughly enjoys the ritual of handshaking which he is beginning to encounter more and more and it occasionally takes the restraining hand of his nanny or mother to still his arm which he waves tirelessly whenever the occasion demands.

He is frequently in trouble with his elders for the usual childhood pranks which have included, if we are to believe the stories in circulation, such simple errors of judgement as dismantling a radio set while his nanny was out of the room; suddenly upending drawers without any warning and spilling their contents over the floor; or jumping exuberantly into the fountain basins on the terrace at Windsor. (The second time he did this, though, he learned his lesson – he failed to notice that someone had turned the water on!)

He has a strong competitive spirit which he puts to use equally purposefully on the football field – where he has demonstrated considerable flair – the skating rink or at play at home. Viscount Linley, the son of Princess Margaret and Lord Snowdon, is one of Andrew's closest friends and the two of them have been re-enacting *Ben Hur* in the grounds of Windsor of late, driving tiny four-wheeled, two-pony carriages (barouches) under the supervision of an instructor. There's also the story of Andrew, brimful of confidence, at the age of four, looking up at his father from his tiny tricycle and challenging him to a race round one of the circular paths in the gardens of Buckingham Palace. Philip agreed and Andrew set off at full speed, his little legs whirling furiously away at the pedals. Philip grabbed Anne's bicycle, which was leaning against a wall, and set off in pursuit. Philip won – but only just.

Early in 1967 Andrew started skating lessons. His instructor said of him after just a few lessons: 'He is a strong, robust little chap . . . quite fearless.' He apparently used to fall rather often but only because he took more risks than other children of his age.

There seems little doubt that Andrew will leave his mark on the world somehow – but perhaps not in the same way as he once left his mark on his father.

Prince Philip came into the nursery to say goodnight to Andrew and his younger brother Edward before going on to a charity film première. He bent over Andrew to kiss him and the little fellow boisterously threw his arms up to clasp his father round the neck. But instead he jabbed a finger into Dad's eye and that night at the cinema Prince Philip arrived with a very painful, swollen left eye.

Prince Edward
Born 10th March 1964
PISCES – Sympathetic, kind, hospitable, compassionate, dependable, and dependent.

EDWARD ANTHONY RICHARD LOUIS, four in March 1968, takes closely after his mother – certainly much more in appearance than his sister or two brothers. He has the same intense expression of the eyes that his mother exhibits from time to time on formal occasions. The eyebrows seem to form into a heavy frown and the face takes on an appearance of deep concentration, bordering on concern or even worry. It is a facial expression that certainly is inherited from the late King George VI and probably his father before him.

Edward has shining fair hair, although it will probably darken as has Andrew's. In public he always appears to be a serious little boy – although at home he is as bubbly and lively as Andrew – and he very much likes to be allowed to get on with things on his own. He took his first few steps unaided when he was fifteen months, and he wasn't much more than two when he was insisting that he could dress himself, no matter how long it took.

Shortly after this he started dancing lessons in the music room at Buckingham Palace, run under the overall supervision of Mme Vacani. It will no doubt not be long before Edward starts lessons with Miss Katherine Peebles, whom Edward learned to call 'Mispy' – all the Royal Family know her by that name – from an early age.

Princess Anne
Born 15th August 1950
LEO – Commanding, frank, generous, poetic, sentimental, incurably romantic, and susceptible to flattery.

ANNE ELIZABETH ALICE LOUISE, twenty-one months younger than her elder brother, has always appeared to her public to be far more forthcoming and uncomplicated than Charles. She seems to smile more often – a dazzling, confident smile that suggests the same breezy informality and charm possessed by her second cousin, Princess Alexandra.

But, on the other hand, she can look serious and even – at times – worried. In their earlier years there seems to be little doubt that Anne wore the trousers in the nursery at Buckingham Palace, but now that the cumulative effects of Charles' wide-ranging experience – Gordonstoun, Timbertop in Australia and now Cambridge, as well as visits to nearly twenty countries – are beginning to take effect on his character and personality, he is becoming increasingly the more dominant in his own unaffected and quiet way.

Anne has been cloistered in the calm, imperturbable, rather detached atmosphere of upper-class education at Benenden School in Kent since September 1963. There she has received the sort of education and grounding that will suit her well for the 'passenger-seat' existence that is probably her fate in life; an education that is a little detached and sheltered from the realities of life as lived by most of her mother's subjects. She passed in six subjects at the Ordinary Level of the GCE examination – one more than Charles – in July 1966 and is now in the middle of a sixth-form course that will possibly take her on to university in 1968 or 1969.

Anne follows fashion trends closely and keeps an up-to-the-minute wardrobe that has included such with-it items of the time as leather jackets, anoraks, rib-knit socks, sloppy jerseys and Beatle caps. In these she can look extremely pert and chic and she obviously revels a little in being able to show her fashion sense to its best effect. But she – like Charles – also suffers at the hands of the Press camera which can catch her in awkward poses or with a pained expression on her face.

She is tall for her age and this extra height and limb length gives her at times the impression of being slightly gauche. But again this is very reminiscent of Alexandra in her teens who has since grown into an elegant, sophisticated woman as, no doubt, will Anne.

But while Anne prides herself on one half of her wardrobe she must surely have reservations about the other – the half she uses for formal occasions. Surely these dresses and suits cannot be her choice? The students of fashion have been appalled by her style on such occasions, which becomes sturdily traditional when she wears what one described as 'motherly dressmaker suits'; and again: 'The handbag she carries is a majestic hold-all more suited to a businesswoman of fifty.'

Marriage is certainly on the horizon for Anne and getting nearer each year. She will probably be one of the most eligible princesses in the 1970s. She is certainly attractive and the matchmakers of the Press were not slow to speculate about how well she and the good-looking Prince Carl Gustav of Sweden appeared to get on when they last met at the wedding of King Constantine of Greece.

But first she has to complete her education and it may well be that in years to come Anne will reveal an interest or a talent that will justify a claim for her in the affections of the British stronger than through being merely Princess Anne, sister of King Charles III.

Viscount Linley
Born 3rd November 1961
SCORPIO – Shrewd, tenacious, firm, determined, frank, energetic and loyal.

DAVID ALBERT CHARLES ARMSTRONG-JONES, six-year-old son of Princess Margaret and Lord Snowdon, is unmistakably his father's son. The facial features are staggeringly Armstrong-Jonesian. His colouring is similar and he has that same little-boy-lost air about him that has made his father such a success with the ladies of his public. He is a lively child with a cheeky grin which inevitably creases his face after Mother calls him by his pet name, 'Popsie', and hands out an admonition for a minor misdemeanour. He has probably sampled the health services of Britain more than any other Royal child. In 1965 he had a succession of accidents and illnesses necessitating a doctor's visit or hospitalisation, including an ear operation, stitches in his chin after he fell from a chair and treatment after he burned himself on an electric fan. And in 1967 he went down with measles and missed – much to his displeasure – Prince Andrew's birthday party at Buckingham Palace. Among the many delights of the party was a Walt Disney film which Viscount Linley, apparently, was particularly upset at missing.

If several recent assignations in Kensington Gardens are anything to go by, David has much of his father's charm. He cut a dashing, bobble-hatted figure sprinting across the gardens on his tricycle to meet some young lady friends.

He sees a lot of Prince Andrew, who is less than two years older. Together they attend the weekly work-outs at a gymnasium in Knightsbridge, dancing lessons at Buckingham Palace (although Andrew no longer goes, probably because he prefers kicking a football around) – David started six weeks before his third birthday – and the occasional swimming parties. He may well be a better swimmer than Andrew – who probably excels in their other activities – because he started three months before him with, among his teachers, his mother, probably the best swimmer in the Royal Family. Both Princess Margaret and the Queen, when they were young girls, won life-saving medals.

David is rather shy when confronted by crowds and on one memorable occasion, when he was serving as page at a society wedding, he doubled back into the church at the sight of the onlookers and had to be persuaded to come back out – which he eventually did – somewhat sheepishly. It is this shyness which will make him, together with the dashing Andrew and the angelic Earl of St Andrews, the debs' delight – unless that species becomes extinct – in 1984; or perhaps it had better be 1983!

Lady Sarah Armstrong-Jones
Born 1st May 1964
TAURUS – Reserved, placid, stubborn, musical, warm-hearted, faithful, devoted and considerate.

SARAH FRANCES ELIZABETH ARMSTRONG-JONES, three last birthday, is a pretty little girl, slightly chubby, and certainly a lot more like her mother than her brother, Viscount Linley. She was named Sarah because it is a favourite name of her parents, Frances after Lord Snowdon's grandmother and Elizabeth after the Queen.

Like her brother she seems very attached to a bobble hat and is frequently to be seen wearing it on walks in Kensington Gardens with her mother or her nanny, Miss Verona Sumner. On these walks they are inevitably accompanied by the family's King Charles Spaniel, Rowley, who is a great friend of Sarah's.

The Earl of St Andrews
Born 26th June 1962
CANCER – Sensitive, unassuming, romantic, sentimental, possessive, easily influenced.

GEORGE PHILIP NICHOLAS, son of the Duke and Duchess of Kent, five last birthday, has a very striking appearance – a handsome head of blond hair, usually immaculately coiffeured, and a bright, intelligent face. He is, indeed, a pretty boy, dressed in an elegant, perhaps slightly precious style, no doubt under the influence of his beautiful mother.

He spent a year in Hong Kong from the age of six months when the Duke, then a captain in the Royal Scots Greys, had been posted there. By the age of one he was crawling energetically round the Kent home in the British Crown Colony. He is a happy-natured boy whose early interests seem to incline towards things mechanical. He is certainly an airplane enthusiast and has several models in his room – and no doubt elsewhere   at the Kent home of Coppins, at Iver, Buckinghamshire. Not long ago, he managed to persuade his parents to take him to Heathrow Airport, London, where he spent a couple of hours watching, fascinated, from the viewing platform as flight after flight landed and took off.

Lady Helen Windsor
Born 28th April 1964
TAURUS – Reserved, placid, stubborn, musical, warm-hearted, faithful, devoted and considerate.

HELEN MARINA LUCY, three last birthday, will probably take strongly after her mother. She already has the same slightly upturned nose and facial moulding. She seems to be a serious little girl whom the camera never manages to catch in a gay mood. She occupies very much the same position as Lady Sarah Armstrong-Jones, being the first daughter but second child, and was, in fact, born three days earlier than Lady Sarah. She, too, is great friends with the dog of the household – in the Kents' case, a large but gentle black Labrador who answers to the name of Flint.

James Ogilvy
Born 29th February 1964
PISCES – Sympathetic, kind, hospitable, compassionate, dependable and dependent.

JAMES ROBERT BRUCE OGILVY, son of Princess Alexandra and the Hon Angus Ogilvy, is the unluckiest of the Royal children. He is the one who had the misfortune to be born on 29th February, 1964, a tragedy in one's earlier years. He weighed an impressive 9lb 6oz at birth and has retained a certain chunkiness since, although he seems to be getting slimmer as time passes. He's an active little fellow who has inherited the sparkling smile of his mother and facial expression of his father.

His arrival set a precedent. It was, according to one expert in such matters, the first time a Royal Princess of Britain had given birth to an untitled son. In 1917 George V decreed that the titles of Prince and Princess could only be taken by the grandchildren of the sovereign in the male line. But there are ways round this. Letters patent under the Great Seal allowed the Queen, or Princess Elizabeth as she was, to pass on the titles to her children, and Princess Margaret was able to because her husband was created an Earl.

Like Prince Andrew, James has shown an early interest in football. On one memorable occasion he was playing with a multi-coloured ball in the garden of the family home, Thatched Lodge, which is situated in Richmond Park on the western outskirts of London. Through the gates he spied a group of pigeons, preening themselves on the ground. With elaborate care, James took careful aim, booted the ball straight through the gates and towards the birds, and, with a cry of 'C-H-I-C-K-E-N-S!', charged the pigeons – only to fall flat on his face and suffer the embarrassment of being led back, in tears, by the friendly policeman on duty, to face his nanny.

14

Both James and his sister, Marina, are fortunate in having a mother like Princess Alexandra who is probably the most informal of Royal mums and the most refreshingly ingenious. She must surely be the only Princess on record anywhere as having ordered fish and chips – expressly in newspaper – for her lunch while sitting under a hairdryer in an expensive West End salon. (Also for the record, she spurned plate, knife and fork, preferring to eat in the traditional manner – with her fingers.)

Miss Marina Ogilvy
Born 31st July 1966
LEO – Commanding, frank, generous, poetic, sentimental, incurably romantic and susceptible to flattery.

MARINA VICTORIA ALEXANDRA OGILVY, not yet eighteen months old, weighed 7lb 8oz at birth – exactly the same as the two children of the Duke and Duchess of Kent, the Earl of St Andrews and Lady Helen Windsor. Her father was present throughout her birth which, according to the statisticians, was probably a precedent among 'Royal' fathers.

She takes the name of Marina from her grandmother, Victoria from the famous Queen, her great-great-grandmother, and Alexandra, of course, from her mother.

Viscount Lascelles
Born 21st October 1950

James Lascelles
Born 5th October 1953

Robert Lascelles
Born 14th February 1955

DAVID HENRY GEORGE, James Edward and Robert Jeremy Hugh are the sons of the Earl of Harewood by his first marriage. They receive little publicity and quite rightly so although they follow immediately in succession to the throne after their father and the two Ogilvy children.

The Lascelles boys, David the eldest at seventeen, James, fourteen, and Robert, nearly thirteen, are a very different breed of children – hardly 'Royal' at all. They are perfectly free to move without the Press going with them. They have no bodyguards or special police attention. They go to lesser public schools – James to Westminster, although his father went to Eton.

They are different from the other Royal children in one other most significant detail. Their vocations are not pre-determined or their existence sheltered. All of them have seen their home disrupted, as it must have been, by the divorce of their parents and, consequently, they have had to adjust to the absence of a father, although he still visits them.

And two of them have seen death. David and James were with their father and their grandmother, the Princess Royal, one early spring day in 1965, when she collapsed and died on a walk in the grounds of Harewood House, near Leeds. Death, in no matter what form, is bound to have an effect on its witnesses – particularly when they are at an impressionable age, as were David and James.

The Lascelles have, in these respects, experienced much more than their Royal relatives are likely to do for a long time. One hopes that they are none the worse for that.

Footnote

This has been a brief, informal glimpse of the thirteen Royal children in immediate line of succession to the British throne. It has attempted to show them as the children they are, capable of tears, temper, sulkiness, cheekiness and, indeed, all the other characteristics that are to be found in children everywhere.

It is, by inference, a gentle appeal for them to be treated as such – both by their parents and their public. They are, after all, only human. To expect them to be more than that is to believe in fairy tales that begin, 'Once upon a time, there lived a handsome Prince . . .', and that is a child's privilege; but every child has to grow up, as do the thirteen pictured in this book. Let us hope that all of them retain the happiness, enthusiasm and zest for life which they exhibit on these pages.

Illustrations

Prince Charles
Prince of Wales
Born 14 November 1948
Scorpio

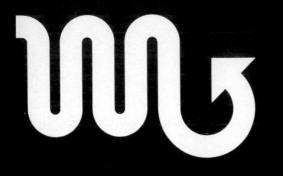

(*Left*) A photograph that superbly illustrates the influence that father has on son. Both in step, both showing the regal trademark of left hand elegantly thrust into jacket pocket, both sporting a half-inch of white handkerchief in breast pocket

The enthusiastic reception Charles received in Australia when he arrived to attend Geelong Grammar School brought from him a reaction rarely, if ever, seen in Britain. This photograph (*above*) shows him almost overwhelmed with the warmth and affection of the Australians

Another photograph of Charles in
Australia, obviously enjoying himself as
he uses a rip-saw at Timbertops, the
bushland section of Geelong Grammar
School

Charles is fast becoming, like his father, an accomplished performer on the polo field. The photograph on the right shows him in a resolute mood, reminiscent of his father, during his competitive début at Windsor Great Park in April 1967 when he distinguished himself by scoring a goal. His team, on this occasion, won by five goals to one-and-a-half

Charles, in casual attire with an Australian-style bush hat, prepares for a river trip on the Rio Grande during his visit to Jamaica in August 1966 for the Commonwealth Games. Princess Anne is standing behind him. They were installed in comfortable armchairs securely attached to large bamboo rafts and were ferried over the Rio Grande rapids

From the sun of Jamaica to the snowy slopes of Liechtenstein where Charles and Anne were guests of Prince Franz Josef II early in 1966, at his castle of Vaduz. Here, Prince Philip watches Charles and Ann toboggan down one of the slopes at Malbun

(*Below, left*) Charles, in tweed sports jacket, on his way to visit The Queen Mother, his grandmother, in the King Edward VII Hospital for Officers, London, during her confinement there in December 1966. (*Far right*) Nine months earlier Charles was wearing very much the same style of jacket when he signed two bibles on his first day at Geelong Grammar School. (*Below, right*) Still in traditional, and rather outdated, dress – double-breasted blazer and wide-bottomed trousers with turn-ups – Charles arrives, with cello, for a concert rehearsal. His style of clothes could well be more modern, perhaps, without sacrificing the restrained elegance to which Charles, as future king, need adhere

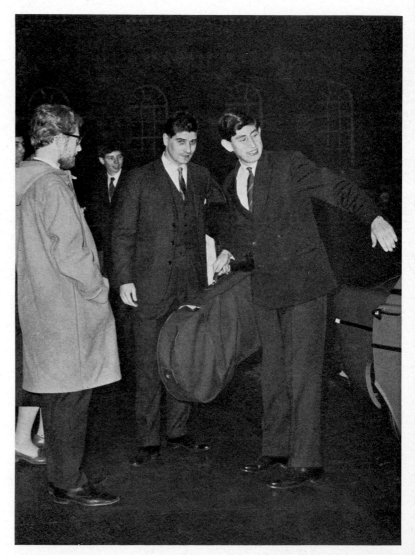

26

Prince Andrew
Born 19 February 1960
Aquarius

Prince Edward
Born 10 March 1964
Pisces

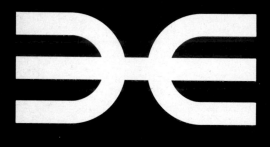

Prince Andrew, as this sequence of photographs shows, is very much the outdoor boy. It also shows him as a soccer player of some promise. The picture at the foot of the opposite page proves him to be a young man with a fine sense of balance, co-ordination and ball control, reminiscent even of a Greaves or a Pele! These photographs were taken in the playground of a school in Chelsea where weekly soccer matches were arranged early in 1967 at which Andrew was a regular player and frequent star

(*Above*) A sturdy Prince Andrew strides the deck of the Royal Yacht *Britannia*. Could he be thinking of the day he will be master of his own sea-going vessel? (*Right*) He sprints across the turf of Smith's Lawn, Windsor, to be first to replace the divots kicked up by polo ponies. While the Queen watched with amusement from the Royal Box, Andrew carried clods of earth around looking for holes in which to put them

(*Above*) Boarding a train for Balmoral Castle: first in is Viscount Linley, Princess Margaret's son, followed by Prince Edward, clutching his mother's hand, Andrew and, just visible, Lady Sarah Armstrong-Jones

(*Above*) Andrew, self-confident and remarkably assured, in the pageboy's uniform he wore for the wedding at Westminster Abbey of the Marquis of Hamilton and Miss Sacha Phillips. (*Left*) A happy wave from the train taking him and brother Charles away to Sandringham for the Royal Family's last Christmas holidays. In all these photographs Andrew exhibits a sturdy independence and self-reliance, surprising, perhaps, in one so young

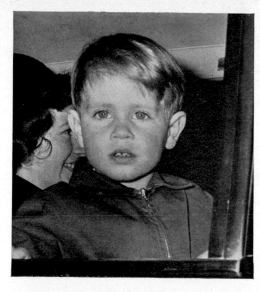

(*Far left*) A charming photograph of the Royal Family, *sans* Edward, after Andrew's assured performance as page-boy at the Westminster Abbey wedding of the Marquis of Hamilton and Miss Sacha Phillips. (*Left*) Prince Edward – 'he has the same intense expression of the eyes as his mother . . . a facial expression inherited from the late King George VI'. (*Below*) Aboard the Royal Train, bound for Balmoral: Andrew looking a trifle dubious, his mother radiant, while Edward (*left*) and Princess Margaret's daughter, Lady Sarah (*right*), just manage to peek out of the window

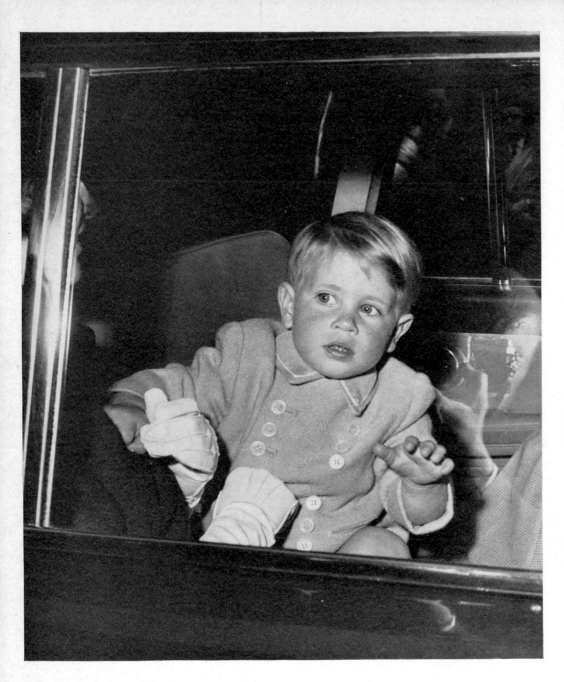

(*Above*) Edward leans forward curiously
in his nanny's arms to present a better
picture for the photographer whose
reflection is mirrored in the car window.
(*Right*) A delightfully informal picture of
Edward and Andrew taken in the grounds
of Buckingham Palace. It succeeds, where
many photographs fail, in capturing
Edward with his impish smile

A young Edward tightly clutching his mother's hand and eager, or so it seemed, to escape into the Royal Train from the battery of photographers present; or perhaps his motive was to get his mother away from all that annoying handshaking and those formal farewells in order to start the summer holiday that much earlier

After the Trooping the Colour ceremony, Her Majesty the Queen points out the fly-past by Lightnings of RAF Bomber Command to an absorbed Edward, who once again has a look of intense concentration on his face

Back to London after the Christmas holidays at Sandringham, with one hand tightly in the grasp of his nanny, and the fingers of the other extended as if they were tinkering at an imaginary keyboard

39

Princess Anne
Born 15 August 1950
Leo

(*Left*) Princess Anne at Liverpool Street Station, London, after the Christmas holidays at Sandringham. Students of fashion would probably have something to say about the combination of knee-length boots, crocheted stockings and the 'sensible' suit. Anne, herself, would probably have something to say about the way she has been caught by the camera – too often newspaper photographs make her appear slightly gauche. But, like her second cousin, Princess Alexandra, who had the same trouble, a more assured elegance will no doubt come with maturity. (*Right*) Caught with a frown on her face at Smith's Lawn after watching her father play in a polo match; but at least this time the attire is casually chic and the pose pleasantly relaxed and informal

For Jamaica it was a cheeky, Beatle-style cap and belted hipsters. This picture was taken just before the Princess and Charles 'shot' the rapids on the Rio Grande

For a horse-jumping open day near her school at Benenden, Kent, jodhpurs, white shirt, tie and a sixpenny ice-cream cornet

For Cowes, aboard the yawl *Bloodhound*, another Beatle cap, jeans and a rugged waterproof jacket that add up to a winning combination. On the evidence of these photographs there seems little doubt that the Princess looks her best and more at ease in casual clothes

45

Anne, looking sophisticated and, if anything, a year or two older than Charles, pictured at the three-day horse trials at Badminton, Gloucestershire

A delightful picture of Anne and Andrew taken at Smith's Lawn, Windsor. Anne's dazzling smile will probably win her as much affection as has Princess Alexandra's for her

The sort of picture that does the Princess little credit. But perhaps the same charge could be levelled against her hair style and her dress, both of which, it has been said, are too old for her. Charles has just come off the polo field for welcome refreshment

An evening out at the theatre. The full-length dress in silk is garter-blue which, together with the fur stole, the dazzling necklace and a sophisticated hair style, made a great impression on those present. At the theatre, the London Aldwych, the Princess saw two *Comédie Française* productions and then was the guest of the French Ambassador in London, together with her mother, father and Prince Charles, at a candlelight supper party

(*Left*) Prince Charles, in three-piece suit, and Princess Anne, at the wedding of the Marquis of Hamilton, at which Prince Andrew was a pageboy. Anne's costume, it was said at the time, did not do her justice

(*Below*) A bent knee at the National Scout Service in April 1967 at St George's Chapel, Windsor, betrays slight fatigue. But, in years to come, Anne will no doubt learn the skill that her mother possesses of being able to stand for long periods absolutely straight and with hardly a movement. Also in the photograph is the Chief Scout of the Commonwealth, Sir Charles Maclean, BT, KBE

Viscount Linley
Born 3 November 1961
Scorpio

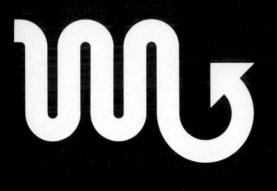

Lady Sarah Armstrong-Jones
Born 1 May 1964
Taurus

David, Viscount Linley, cuts 'a dashing, bobble-hatted figure sprinting across Kensington Gardens on his tricycle to meet some young lady friends'. After preliminary discussion (*right, above*), possibly concerning the nanny who signalled right and turned left immediately in front of him on his way across the Gardens, he demonstrates his prowess and climbing ability on one of the Gardens' gates

A charming picture (*right*) of David, Viscount Linley, on his way to Prince Edward's birthday party. There is the eager expectation of cream cakes and jelly and ice cream in that happy smile. (*Below*, *right*) David (*extreme right*), with his sister, Lady Sarah Armstrong-Jones, and Prince Edward, on their way to Sandringham to celebrate the New Year

(*Below*) In among Royal skirts and ankles, David and Sarah await transport to take them home to Clarence House after summer holidays at Balmoral Castle

(*Right*) A little boy, a big car and a row of bearskins. David watches the Guards' band as he leaves Buckingham Palace after lessons there. The face at the window is not identified

David, with his nanny, stands at the side entrance to his home, Clarence House, to watch the Queen's Guard march past to St James's Palace. The mystique and fascination that the soldier in uniform, particularly traditional uniform, has for most small boys is beautifully depicted in this photograph

A delightful photograph of Lady Sarah, apparently saluting, on her way to Prince Edward's birthday party. She has the wide-eyed look of her father, but does not so closely resemble him as does David

Outside a gymnasium in Knightsbridge,
London, one day, a little girl (Lady
Sarah) was waiting for her big brother
(Viscount Linley). He went regularly to
the gymnasium to keep fit and agile.
Suddenly, he appeared at the door, with
a stern expression on his face. Ah,
thought the little girl, now perhaps we
can go home for tea. But her big brother
was not ready for tea. Flexing the muscles
that he had been exercising in the
gymnasium, he decided to try them out
on a friend of his. Oh dear, thought the
little girl, as she watched her big brother.
I wish he wouldn't do that. We will be
late for tea

David and Sarah with a beach all to themselves. It was a little overwhelming at first – where to start work, with all the beach to choose from; what to build, with Father suggesting a sand castle and Mother a ring of sand pies; and who was to do what. But it didn't take long for buckets and spades to be fully employed. These pictures were taken on the Sussex coast during a recent family holiday

The Earl of St Andrews
Born 26 June 1962
Cancer

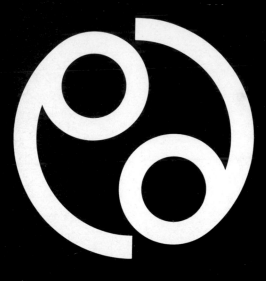

Lady Helen Windsor
Born 28 April 1964
Taurus

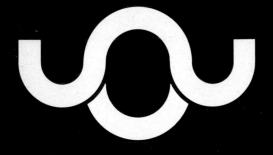

(*Below*) George, Earl of St Andrews, about to go for a drive with his mother, the Duchess of Kent, his extremely blond hair pushing its way out from beneath the balaclava

(*Right*) George arrives with his mother for his first day at school in Datchet, a small town near Windsor and not far from the Kents' home of Coppins, at Iver, Buckinghamshire. Flint, the family's Labrador, is just visible on the right of the picture

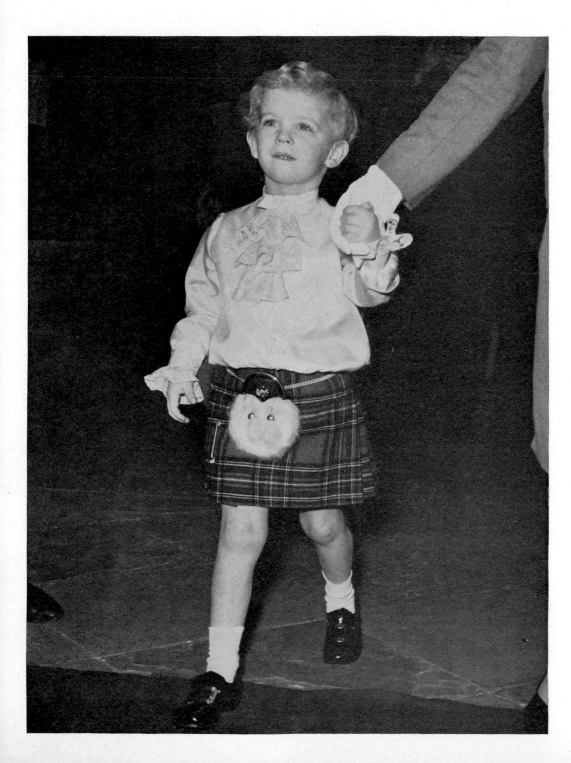

Like Prince Andrew, the Earl of St Andrews is also called upon for page duty at weddings. These two photographs show him in tartan kilt at the London wedding of Miss Fiona Bowes-Lyon, whose father is a cousin of the Queen Mother, and Mr Joseph Goodhart. It is not a yawn that George is giving on the opposite page, but a lusty yell which he let out after the ceremony

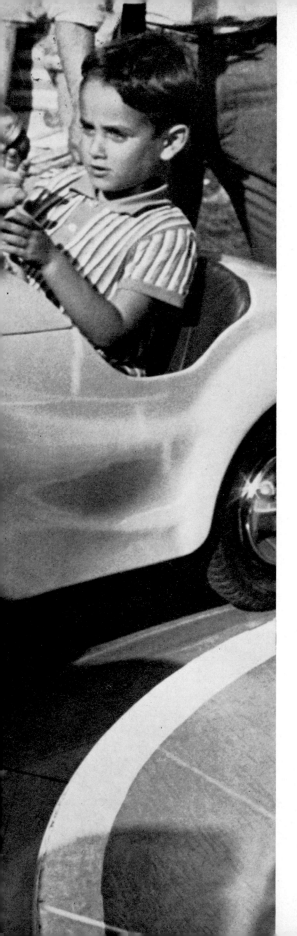

Things mechanical appear to interest George, not least among them cars . . . whether they be the merry-go-round variety at Iver village fête, or his father's Mini. The picture below shows George as the good-looking young lad he is and the eligible young man he will be in fifteen years' time

Lady Helen Windsor is an attractive little
girl with the same facial moulding and
slightly snub nose as her mother. Her
hair is fair, rather than the blond of her
brother's. These photographs were taken
on a warm spring day outside the Kent
home of Coppins. Lady Helen showed
much care and attention over the arrange-
ment of the dolls in their pram, constantly
attended by the faithful Flint, the
Labrador that can be seen in the back-
ground of the photograph to the right

The village fair at Iver in Buckinghamshire is a great attraction for the children
in the neighbourhood, not least for
George and Helen. We have already seen
them trying the merry-go-round (*page* 70);
here, with their father and mother, they
watch the judging of the beauty contest.
Helen seems to be a serious little girl
whom the camera can never catch in a gay
mood. Her mother's gaiety and effer-
vescence will probably emerge as she
grows older

James Ogilvy
Born 29 February 1964
Pisces

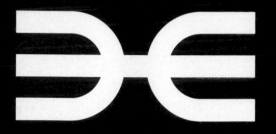

Miss Marina Ogilvy
Born 31 July 1966
Leo

Master James Ogilvy is, like Prince Andrew, an enthusiastic footballer, although as yet without the maturer skills that the Queen's young son shows. On this occasion, James was playing football at his home, Thatched Lodge, in the grounds of Richmond Park, on the south-western outskirts of London. He picked up the ball, kicked it in the air, dribbled it round a water hydrant . . .

. . . saw a group of pigeons strutting a few yards ahead of him, took careful aim, booted the ball straight at them, charged after it uttering a blood-curdling cry of 'C-H-I-C-K-E-N-S!' . . . and fell flat on his face. He then had to suffer the embarrassment of being picked up by the policeman on duty and carried back to the arms of his nanny

(*Above*) Miss Marina Ogilvy, in the arms of her mother, on the day of her christening at the Chapel Royal, St James's Palace, London. (*Right*) A beaming smile for the camera from a proud James as Marina takes the air in her pram

(*Right*) James plays hopscotch over the flagstones of the front path at Thatched Lodge before he says goodbye to his mother and father at the gate. (*Extreme right*) James, with Marina in the arms of their nanny, on his way to a birthday party for him held at the home of the Duke and Duchess of Kent. On this occasion, James' parents were travelling abroad

On the day of Marina's christening at the Chapel Royal, St James's Palace, her mother looked radiant and James, taking a lead from his elegant father, looked calm and relaxed, although he did occasionally show the natural curiosity of a boy of his age, peeping this way, then that, and tugging every so often at his father's hand. Marina was christened Marina Victoria Alexandra. The first name after her grandmother, the second after her great-great-grandmother, the famous Queen, and Alexandra after her own mother. The photograph on the right shows the family outside Thatched Lodge about to leave for the Chapel Royal

Viscount Lascelles
Born 21 October 1950
Libra

James Lascelles
Born 5 October 1953
Libra

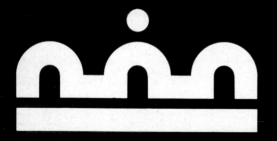

Robert Lascelles
Born 14 February 1955
Aquarius

The photograph on page 89 shows David, Viscount Lascelles with his father. The photographs on these two pages show him (*above*) with the late Princess Royal, his grandmother, and his mother at Harewood House, Yorkshire, the family home. David, just seventeen, was eight when this photograph was taken. (*Right*) David with his mother, holding Robert, now nearing his thirteenth birthday, and his father, who has James on his knee. James is sixteen months older than Robert

The photographs on these two pages, and on 92 and 93, were taken before the divorce and remarriage of the Earl of Harewood. They are included only because they are the best photographs available of three rarely photographed young men who, like all their relatives pictured in this book, are in immediate line of succession to the throne

David and James with their parents at the
Battersea Pleasure Gardens in 1960. The
boys had just won prizes at roll-a-ball

David with his parents in March 1961
when he and his mother went to London
Airport to say goodbye to the Earl of
Harewood. He was flying to Moscow to
discuss arrangements for the 1962
Edinburgh Festival

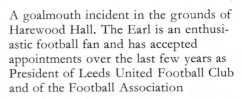

A goalmouth incident in the grounds of
Harewood Hall. The Earl is an enthusiastic football fan and has accepted
appointments over the last few years as
President of Leeds United Football Club
and of the Football Association